LEARN

CARE

TRAIN

LOVE

HAVE FUN

A COMPLETE GUIDE FOR KIDS

This book brings up the responsibility of owning a corgi to all young enthusiasts, as an educational process. Understanding the unique characteristics of the breed is the first step, followed by daily care and instructions on how to play-train a corgi puppy at home.

My corgi and I thank you for the order, she has just wagged his tail.
Please let us know how you like our book at
theapubincolors@gmail.com

# TABLE OF CONTENTS

# WHY DO YOU LOVE CORGIS?

_____

_____

_____

_____

_____

_____

_____

_____

_____

_____

_____

_____

# WHY DO YOU LOVE CORGIS?

_____

_____

_____

_____

_____

_____

_____

_____

_____

_____

_____

**DID YOU KNOW?**

## ORIGIN

Ancient herding breed originated in Wales, UK

## ROYAL COMPANIONS

Queen Elizabeth II owned more than 30 corgies

## SIZE

Corgis are small to medium-sized dogs

## THE LIFESPAN OF A CORGI

12-15 years of joy

## INTELLIGENT AND TRAINABLE

Intelligent and quick learners, they excel in obedience and agility training.

## BIG PERSONALITY AND VOCAL NATURE

They are often described as brave, vigilant, and energetic dogs. Different barks and vocalizations are used by corgis to communicate with their owners.

## WEIGHT

They are small dogs but can grow to be around 27 pounds.

## LOYALTY

They are very loyal and will follow their owners everywhere.

## SOCIAL DOGS

Corgis are generally friendly and sociable with other animals and people. They like interacting with people and meeting new furry and human companions.

## WEATHER-RESISTANT COAT

Their thick fur helps protect corgis from harsh climates. They do, however, favor cool temperatures.

## BIG APPETITE

The love for food that corgis have is well known, and they can develop a tendency to overeat.

## ENDLESS ENERGY

Corgis need regular exercise to stay happy and healthy because they have a very high level of energy.

## GENTLE ATTITUDE

Because of their kind nature, corgis are typically patient and tolerant with children. They frequently have a strong natural urge to look out for and guard their human family members, especially young children.

### AREN'T CORGIS COOL OR WHAT?

# *DID YOU KNOW?*

## CORGI, A SPECIAL BREED

### CORGI PEMBROKE

They have a robust appearance, short legs, and a fox-like face, giving them a foxy look. Their tail is usually docked or naturally short.

### CORGI CARDIGAN

Compared to the Pembroke, they have a longer body, longer tail, and larger ears. They have more rounded fac features.

# DID YOU KNOW?

## TWO ALIKE, YET DIFFERENT

### CORGI CARDIGAN

Long tail 🐾
Variety of colors 🐾

Older Breed: with a history dating back over 3,000 years 🐾

Versatility: they excel in herding, guarding, and even as therapy dogs 🐾

Body Structure: have a slightly larger with a more muscular appearance 🐾

### CORGI PEMBROKE

Docked tail 🐾
Foxy color 🐾

More common and popular worldwide 🐾

Stronger instincts for herding: historically, they have been utilized to handle cattle and other types of livestock. 🐾

Agility: They are known for their agility and speed 🐾

## PET VS. SHOW DOG

### CORGI SHOW DOG

Dogs that are show quality are usually well-bred and adhere to the breed standards that are established by kennel groups or breed organizations. These requirements cover a dog's physical attributes, temperament, and other qualities that qualify it to participate in conformation contests, obedience trials, agility contests, or other canine sports.

### CORGI AS PET

Companion dogs are not required to adhere to any particular breed requirements, they are kept only for company. This is why they can be  more affordable.

12

# QUICK CORGI QUIZ

1.True or False: Pembroke and Cardigan are both types of Corgis

2.How many Corgi breeds are there?
a) One b) Two c) Three

3.Which Corgi breed is more commonly seen with a naturally short or docked tail?
a) Pembroke b) Cardigan

4.Which Corgi breed is known for having a longer body and larger ears?
a) Pembroke b) Cardigan

5.True or False: Both Pembroke and Cardigan Corgis are excellent herding dogs.

6.If I want a corgi as a pet, what should I choose?
a) Corgi in breed standards b) Any corgi

# COLOR YOUR FAVORITE CORGI

# DO YOU KNOW MORE?

_____

_____

_____

_____

_____

_____

_____

_____

_____

_____

_____

_____

# DO YOU KNOW MORE?

PUPPY

# PREPARE YOUR HOME

Getting your house ready for a dog Corgi entails a secure and comfortable environment, so your new furry buddy can flourish.

## REMEMBER

Since every puppy is different, it's critical to provide each one specific attention and care depending on their particular needs. Your Corgi puppy will have the finest start in their new life with you if your home is ready and filled with love.

# PREPARE YOUR HOME 🏠

## PUPPY-PROOFING

Corgi puppies are curious and energetic, so it's crucial to keep dangerous substances and objects out of their reach, protect electrical connections, and restrict access to places where they might be at risk. Make sure garbage cans are locked and keep poisonous plants, chemicals, and prescriptions out of their access.

# PREPARE YOUR HOME

## CREATE A SAFE SPACE

Create a special spot in your house where your Corgi may feel protected. This may be a playpen for puppies, a comfy bed, or a crate. Ensure that it is cozy, well-ventilated, and shielded from drafts.

# PREPARE YOUR HOME

## SAFETY GATES AND FENCING

If you have a backyard, make sure it is completely fenced in to keep your Corgi from getting lost or coming across any dangers. Look for any openings or spaces where they might slip through. Use safety gates to limit access to any stairs you may have until your puppy is mature enough to safely utilize them.

# PREPARE YOUR HOME

## GENTLE PUPPY HANDS

Because puppies are so tender, it's crucial to be gentle when handling and petting them. Be gentle with your strokes while playing. If you love them a lot, they'll become your best friends.

## BOUNDARIES AND RESPECT

Puppies also require their own space. Find out when the puppy needs to nap or spend some time alone in their bed, then offer them some quiet time. It's crucial to respect their privacy and refrain from disturbing them while they're eating or sleeping.

# PREPARE YOUR HOME

## FAMILY PREPARATION

Puppies are learning just like you! Even though they might occasionally make mistakes, it's crucial to have patience and understanding. When they do something nice, shower them with affection, compliments, and treats.

A puppy need a team to care for it. Discuss responsibility sharing with your family. The effort will make it simpler and more enjoyable!

# SHARING TASKS WITH YOUR FAMILY

## MORNING

Feeding and watering

## AFTERNOON

Walking or playtime

## EVENING

Training or practicing commands

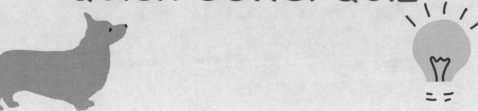

# QUICK CORGI QUIZ

1. What does "puppy-proofing" mean?
   a) Train a corgi to be well-behaved
   b) Making sure the home is safe for a puppy
   c) Choosing the right food for a puppy

2. Why is it important to create a safe space for a puppy?
   a) Puppies need their own area to play in
   b) It keeps the puppy away from other pets
   c) A safe space provides comfort and security for the puppy

3. What are some necessary supplies you need for a puppy?
   a) Food and water bowl, a collar, and a leash
   b) Friends and toys for the puppy to play with
   c) Special food for puppies

4. What does "family preparation" mean when getting a puppy?
   a) Making sure everyone in the family knows how to take care of the puppy
   b) Train the puppy to sit and roll over
   c) Taking the puppy on family adventures

# CORGI CARE
## CHECKLIST

- 🐾 Food and water bowl
- 🐾 Proper collar and leash
- 🐾 Find a reputable veterinarian
- 🐾 Grooming - brushes
- 🐾 Nail trimming - nail clippers
- 🐾 Teeth cleaning supplies
- 🐾 Flea and tick prevention
- 🐾 Heartworm prevention
- 🐾 Research for puppy training classes

# CORGI CARE

## CHECKLIST

### ADD MORE

# YOUR DAILY SCHEDULE
## MAKE TIME FOR YOUR CORGI

# YOUR DAILY SCHEDULE
## MAKE TIME FOR YOUR CORGI

# CORGI'S FOOD

## FEEDING GUIDELINES

Corgis are food lovers. If given the chance, they have a tendency to overeat, therefore it's crucial to have a consistent feeding plan. The best dog food, whether dry, wet, or a combination of both, will be chosen by your vet along with the proper serving size.

NO COOKED BONES

NO CHOCOLATE

NO GRAPES AND RAISINS

NO ONIONS AND GARLIC

NO AVOCADO

NO PIZZA

29

# CORGI'S FOOD

## TRANSITIONING TO A NEW HOME

Maintaining consistency in a Corgi's diet is crucial when moving them from a kennel to your house. Try to stick with the same or a comparable meal at first if the Corgi was previously eating a certain brand or variety. If switching to a new food is unavoidable, do so gradually by combining small portions of the new food with the old one over a few days to prevent digestive distress.

# CORGI'S FOOD

## MEALTIME ROUTINE

For the benefit of Corgis, a regular eating schedule should be established. To aid in regulating their digestion and to foster a sense of order and security, feed them at the same time every day. Don't feed them human food because doing so could cause intestinal problems or bad eating habits.

## RESPECT FOR MEALTIME

While a dog is eating, it should not be disturbed since this may result in stress or guarding behaviors.

# CORGI'S FOOD

## HYDRATION IS VITAL

Make sure your Corgi always has access to fresh water. Watch how much water they are drinking, especially when it's hot outside or they are exercising more. In order to maintain their general health and wellbeing, they must drink enough water.

Bring a water bottle with you wherever you go on family outings, to the beach, or on walks with your corgi.

Avoid letting your corgi quench its thirst in puddle of water, ponds, lakes or any other standing water, unless is absolutely necessary.

# CORGI'S FOOD

## TREATS

Treats are special snacks that we give to dogs to show them love and reward them for good behavior. Given that Corgis are a tiny breed, pick wholesome treats that are small and bite-sized. As a result, they are less likely to overeat or choke. During training sessions, prizes like treats are frequently given. You may reward your Corgi when they learn a new command or behave well by giving them a treat.

33

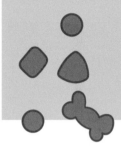

# CORGI'S FOOD

## FOOD ALLERGIES

### WHAT ARE ALLERGIES?

An inappropriate immune response to certain food elements is known as a food allergy.

### SYMPTOMS

- Itching and scratching, especially around the face, ears, paws, and rear end
- Red and inflamed skin
- Frequent ear infections
- Digestive issues like diarrhea, vomiting, or excessive gas
- Poor coat condition or excessive shedding

# CORGI'S FOOD

## FOOD ALLERGIES

## COMMON ALLERGENS

Dogs, particularly Corgis, are more susceptible to food allergies when certain components are present.

- Wheat
- Soy
- Corn
- Other cereals
- Beef
- Dairy products
- Chicken
- Eggs

Remember, if you suspect your Corgi has a food allergy, it's best to consult with a veterinarian for proper diagnosis and guidance. They can provide you with specific recommendations tailored to your Corgi's needs and help you manage their food allergies effectively. 35

# QUICK CORGI QUIZ

1. True or False: It is safe for dogs to eat chocolate.
2. True or False: Grapes or raisins are healthy snacks for dogs.
3. True or False: Onions and garlic can be harmful to dogs.
4. True or False: Corgis have a tendency to overeat if given the chance.
5. What is the importance of establishing a regular feeding schedule for a Corgi?
   a) It helps with their dental health
   b) It prevents them from gaining weight
   c) It regulates their digestion and provides structure
6. How should you handle feeding your dog treats?
   a) Give them as many treats as they want throughout the day
   b) Use treats as a reward during training sessions
   c) Only give treats on special occasions

# MAKE A LIST WITH DOG FOOD

# MAKE A LIST WITH DOG FOOD

### GROOMING NEEDS

Prepare yourself for routine grooming sessions and possible fur cleanup around the house.

The best part: Corgis stay incredibly clean because they shed.

The double coat on corgis needs to be groomed frequently to stay in good shape. To reduce shedding, this entails brushing their fur.

Additionally, Corgis shed sporadically throughout the year and more heavily as the seasons change.

# STRENGTHS AND WEAKNESSES

## BARKING

Yes, Corgis are known to bark frequently. They have a natural tendency to be vocal and may bark in various situations:

**ALERTNESS**

**FEAR OR ANXIETY**

**TERRITORIAL BEHAVIOR**

**BOREDOM OR ATTENTION-SEEKING**

**SEPARATION ANXIETY**

Examining the situation and underlying causes of your Corgi's barking is crucial. It is advised to consult a professional dog trainer or a veterinarian if the barking becomes excessive, obtrusive, or is upsetting you or your Corgi.

# STRENGTHS AND WEAKNESSES

## WHAT iS WiTH THOSE EARS?

### EARS SHAPE

The ears of corgis are normally medium in size, pointed, and upright. Their ears can move and turn to pick up noises coming from various directions since they are mobile.

### SENSITIVITY TO NOISE

Corgis have excellent hearing. Their ears are built to pick up a wide range of sounds, even high-frequency noises that people might not be able to hear. Although this power is amazing, it may also be unsettling.

# STRENGTHS AND WEAKNESSES

## WHAT IS WITH THOSE EARS?

### HANDLING NOISE

While Corgis have excellent hearing, but how they respond to noise depends on their personalities and upbringing. Some Corgis might be more readily startled by loud or unexpected noises, while others might be more used to diverse sounds.

### NOISE MANAGEMENT

Your Corgi needs a secure, peaceful place to hide out when they feel overpowered by noise.

When there is noise around, provide constructive diversions like fun toys or snacks.

## STRENGTHS AND WEAKNESSES

## VET CHECKS

# TAKING CARE OF YOUR FURRY FRIEND

Like any other breed of dog, corgis also need routine veterinary care, vaccines, and preventive measures including flea and tick control, frequent checkups, and dental treatment.

Unfortunately, they are more susceptible to illnesses like intervertebral disc disease, hip dysplasia, and eye problems. Up to the age of 1 year, it is recommended not to let your corgi puppy jump from a great height. Frequent climbing down stairs should also be avoided.

# QUICK CORGI QUIZ

1. How often should you groom a
Corgi's coat?
a) Every day
b) Once a week
c) Once a month
d) Only when it gets dirty

2. True or False: Corgis are generally quiet
and rarely bark.
3. True or False: Excessive barking in Corgis
is often a sign of boredom or lack of mental
stimulation.

4. True or False: Corgis have the ability to
block out noise and remain calm in noisy
situations.
5. True or False: Creating a safe and quiet
space can help Corgis cope with noise-related
stress.
6. True or False: Regular veterinary checkups and vaccinations are essential for keeping
a Corgi healthy.

# STRENGTHS AND WEAKNESSES

## YOUR NOTES

# STRENGTHS AND WEAKNESSES

## YOUR NOTES

_____

_____

_____

_____

_____

_____

_____

_____

_____

_____

_____

# PLAY, PLAY AND PLAY AGAIN

## EXERCISE AND ENERGY LEVELS

Corgi ownership may be both enjoyable and challenging at times. Prepare to provide your Corgi with daily walks, fun, and mental stimulation.

Being an active breed, corgis require regular exercise to keep their weight in check and avoid boredom-related problems. Lack of exercise can lead to weight gain, frustration, and potential health problems.

For sure, You will have an engaged play partner and a lot of fun together.

# PLAY, PLAY AND PLAY AGAIN

## TIME AND ATTENTION

Remember, saying that a corgi wants a lot of interaction? Well, being social animals, they benefit greatly from human company. They require daily play, exercise, and mental stimulation.

But, be careful! Your Corgi may experience separation anxiety or behave destructively if you have a hectic schedule or are unable to give them enough time.

## KEEP THEM ACTIVE!

# HOW TO PLAY?

## FETCH

Playing fetch with a corgi can be a terrific method to get them engaged because they naturally have a chasing and retrieving nature. Throw a frisbee, ball, or other object for them to find  or catch and return back to you.

## TUG-OF-WAR:

Corgis enjoy playing tug of war. Use a tug toy made especially for dogs or a strong rope toy. To ensure supervised and safe play, don't forget to create rules and boundaries.

# HOW TO PLAY?

## AGILITY COURSES

Create a small agility course with tunnels, cones, and hurdles in your backyard or a roomy indoor space. Encourage your Corgi to jump, crawl, and negotiate obstacles as you lead them through the course.

## TRAINING GAMES

Playtime and training sessions should be combined to teach new tricks and reinforce existing commands. Use tactics for positive reinforcement, and give your Corgi goodies or praise when they show desirable behaviour.

# ADD MORE GAMES

# ADD MORE GAMES

# ADD MORE GAMES

# ADD MORE GAMES

# COMMENDS & TRICKS

COME
DOWN

WATCH ME
FIND IT

LEAVE IT
WAIT

PLAY DEAD

PATIENCE

PRACTICE

FUN

# COMMENDS & TRICKS

## COME

Keeps your pup out of trouble.

From a distance, pull the leash in your direction and call the dog to come. Praise or treat it affectionately when it begins to move and approaches you. Be patient and keep doing this for a few days until it learns the command.

## DOWN

Give your pet a treat firstly. Gently approach its nose and face while holding that in a closed palm. By gradually lowering your hand to the floor, you can allow it to follow you as the dog sniffs. Give the down command once your pet is lying down by continuing to slide your hand down to the floor. Appreciate your pup good conduct with a treat. Replicate several times.

# COMMENDS & TRICKS

## LEAVE IT

A dog should not ingest anything or attempt to grab any potentially harmful objects.

In both hands, hold the treats. Move the first hand gradually so that the pup licks or sniffs it before telling to leave it. Take away the first treat when it tries to take it from your hand. Using the other hand, give it a second treat when it becomes disinterested in the first. That demonstrates how well your dog has executed the required behavior. Regular practice will help your dog become proficient.

# COMMENDS & TRICKS

## WAIT

When is meal time, have your dog sit and tell it to Wait!
Take a treat out of the food bowl and give it to your corgi while holding the bowl at shoulder height. You can do this with your corgi's regular food or you can use treats that your dog enjoys the most.

## WATCH ME

Give to the pup a treat in your closed hand and bring your hand up to its face and nose. Say the command once you have its entire attention and have established eye contact. Give it a treat as a reward. When you take your dog to a busy place, this guidance will be helpful.

# COMMENDS & TRICKS

## FIND IT

Present a toy or treat while the dog is waiting, and let the corgi to sniff it. After that, move to a different room or area of your yard and place the toy or some treats around.  Make it simple at first by leaving them partially visible.  Tell your dog "find it!" and give him some help, if needed.

## PLAY DEAD

With the dog in the down position, hold a treat close to your dog's nose, and slowly pull it over to its side so it will have to roll onto its side to get it. As soon as your dog is lying on its side, say "good" and give him a treat. After that, move your hand toward the dog's opposite shoulder and say "Play Dead!".

59

# HAVE YOU CHOSEN THE PERFECT NAME FOR YOUR CORGI? MAKE A LIST

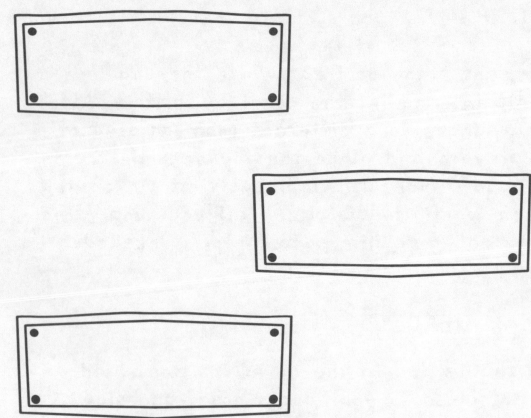

# YOUR FAVOURITE
# TRICKS

# YOUR FAVOURITE TRICKS

# YOUR FAVOURITE TRICKS

# YOUR FAVOURITE TRICKS

# DON'TS

## DON'T PULL THEIR TAILS OR EARS!

Because Corgis have delicate ears and tails, pulling or tugging on them should be avoided to prevent pain and suffering for the canine.

## DON'T APPROACH THEM TOO QUICKLY!

Corgis are easily frightened, it is essential to approach them quietly and gently. They could become frightened or anxious if you run toward them or make loud noises.

# DON'TS

## DON'T PLAY TOO ROUGHLY!

Corgis enjoy playing, but if it gets too rough, they can easily get hurt. You and your friends should refrain from playing games that require biting or aggressive behavior, such as wrestling.

## DON'T LEAVE THEM UNSUPERVISED!

When children are playing with a corgi, adult supervision is necessary to safeguard the safety of both the child and the dog. It's crucial to watch after corgis at all times because they have a propensity for being nosy and mischievous.

# NOTES & PAWS

# NOTES & PAWS

# NOTES & PAWS

# NOTES & PAWS

## DON'T FORGET

Having a dog as a companion is a big responsibility and will last a long time.

# REFERANCES

1. The Corgi Guide by the Happy
   Puppy Site - thehappypuppysite.com

2. American Kennel Club (AKC) -
akc.org

3. The Pembroke Welsh Corgi Club of
America - pwcca.org

4. "The Complete Guide to Corgis:
Everything You Need to Know to Bring
Home Your First Corgi" by David
Anderson

5. "Corgis: The Ultimate Guide for
Corgi Lovers" by Tara Adams

Elizabeth T. Milson

Made in United States
Troutdale, OR
12/23/2023

16380528R00042